D1533257

Mahatma Gandhi

Terry Barber

ACTIVIST SERIES

WITHDRAWN
Quick Reads

Funded by a
California Library Literacy Services
(CLLS) grant

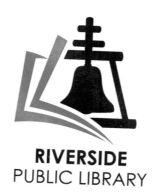

RIVERSIDE
PUBLIC LIBRARY

Gandhi travels by train.

Gandhi's Decision

It is 1893. Gandhi rides on a train in South Africa. The train chugs into the night. Gandhi sits in first class. The train stops. A white man gets on the train. He sees Gandhi. The white man says, "Get out of here."

Gandhi, age 26 years

Gandhi's Decision

Gandhi is Indian. Indian people cannot ride in first class. Gandhi will not leave his seat. The police throw Gandhi off the train. Gandhi spends a long, cold night in the train station. This night changes Gandhi's life.

Gandhi is 24 years old.

Africa

South Africa

Gandhi's Decision

Gandhi sits in the train station. He thinks about his future. He needs to make a decision. Should he fight for Indians' rights in South Africa? Or should he return home to India? He decides to fight for Indians' rights.

Gandhi stays in South Africa for 21 years.

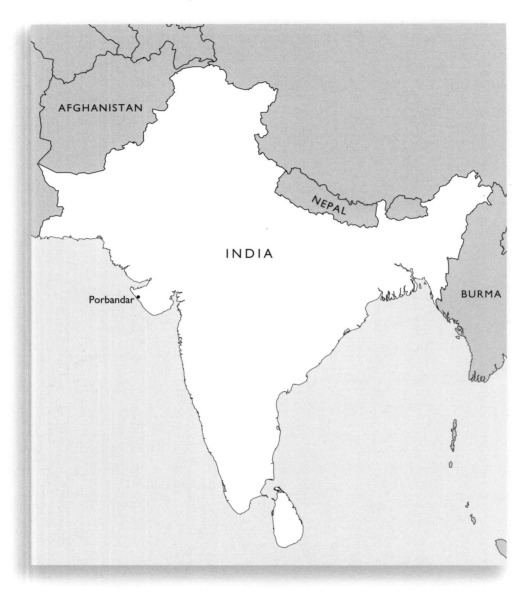

Gandhi is born in Porbandar, India.

Early Years

Gandhi is born in India in 1869. He is a shy, quiet child. Gandhi starts school at age seven. He works hard. He is an average student. Gandhi does not like sports. He likes to take long walks by himself.

Gandhi's full name at birth is Mohandas Karamchand Gandhi.

Gandhi, age 7 years

A Hindu wedding in 1887.

Early Years

Gandhi's family are Hindus. In the 1800s, most Hindus marry at a young age. Gandhi's parents choose his wife. Her name is Kasturba. Gandhi and Kasturba marry in 1882. They are both 13 years old. Their first child is born in 1886.

Gandhi and Kasturba are married for 62 years.

Kasturba in 1902

Gandhi's mother, Putlibai

Early Years

Gandhi wants to study law in England. Gandhi's mother does not want him to go. Gandhi makes three promises. He will not eat meat or drink alcohol. And he will not have sex in England. Gandhi sails to India at age 19.

Gandhi's wife and son stay in India.

Gandhi sits in front of his law office.

Life in South Africa

Gandhi gets his law degree in 1891. He sails home to India. There are not many jobs with law firms. Gandhi cannot find good work in India. He finds work in South Africa. He also finds **racism** in South Africa.

Gandhi works as a lawyer in South Africa.

Gandhi sits with the Natal Indian Congress, 1895.

Life in South Africa

White people rule South Africa. They pass racist laws. Indian people cannot own property. Indian people cannot stay in white hotels. Indian people pay higher taxes than white people. Indian people do not have equal rights in South Africa.

Gandhi forms the Natal Indian Congress in 1894.

Gandhi's Beliefs

Gandhi wants to make life better for
Indians. He wants to learn how to
fight racism. He reads holy books.
He learns from the different religions.
Gandhi learns that peaceful ways can
bring change.

Gandhi
reads the
Bible, the Koran,
and other holy
books.

Gandhi writes: There is no God but truth.

Gandhi's Beliefs

Many leaders use violence to make change. Gandhi is different. He believes in non-violence and truth. Gandhi calls these two beliefs **satyagraha**. This word means truth-force. Gandhi believes that truth and non-violence are strong forces. These forces can lead to change.

Satyagraha is pronounced sat-ya-gra-ha.

Gandhi lives in this hut.

Gandhi's Beliefs

Gandhi believes a simple life leads to harmony. Gandhi changes his life. He gives up his wealth. He gives up his home. He gives up his fine clothes. Gandhi begins to live a simple life.

Gandhi owns only these items.

Gandhi cuts vegetables at the ashram.

Gandhi's Beliefs

Gandhi starts an **ashram** in 1904. The ashram is a community. People live and work together on a farm. People build a simple life on the farm. They grow their own food. They make their own furniture.

The ashram community, 1905

Gandhi sits in a South African prison.

Gandhi's Beliefs

Gandhi leads many **protests** in South Africa. He protests racist laws. He gets Indians to go on strike. He wins the Indians more rights. Gandhi is beaten for being a leader. Gandhi is put in jail for being a leader.

In 1914, South Africa's new laws give Indians basic rights.

Gandhi travels in India by train.

Life in India

In 1915, Gandhi returns to India. He is a hero. He is famous for his work in South Africa. Gandhi travels around India for a year. He learns about India's problems. He sees poverty and hunger. Gandhi wants to see change in India.

People give Gandhi the name Mahatma, which means great soul.

The untouchables are the poorest of the poor.

The untouchables clean the streets.

Life in India

Hindus are born into different **castes** or social groups. The lowest caste is called the **untouchables**. They do not have any rights. Gandhi believes India's caste system is a problem. Gandhi tells Indians to treat the untouchables as equals.

Gandhi gives the untouchables a new name: Harijan. This means "The Children of God."

The
British rule
India from 1858
to 1947.

Life in India during British rule.

Gandhi's Protests

The British rule India. The British treat Indians like second-class citizens. Gandhi wants to free India from British rule. Gandhi believes Indians must depend upon themselves. Indians must solve the problems of India. Gandhi starts to protest British rule.

Gandhi becomes a leader of the Indian National Congress in 1919.

Gandhi works at his spinning wheel.

Gandhi's Protests

Gandhi boycotts British goods. He tells Indians to boycott British clothes. Gandhi leads the way. He spins 200 yards of thread every day. In the 1920s, Indians learn to spin and weave. The spinning wheel becomes a **symbol** of protest.

The Indians weave thread on a handloom to make fabric.

Several
thousand
Indians march
200 miles to
the sea.

Gandhi leads the salt march in 1930.

Gandhi's Protests

Gandhi protests British laws. The Salt Acts do not allow Indians to gather and sell salt. Gandhi leads a 24-day march to the sea. Gandhi reaches the sea. He picks up a few grains of salt. This simple act is a symbol of protest.

Kastburba's last moments.

Gandhi's Protests

Gandhi leads a big protest against British rule in 1942. The British send Gandhi and Kasturba to prison. Kasturba gets sick and dies in Gandhi's arms. A part of Gandhi dies with her. Gandhi leaves prison in 1944. He keeps working for India's freedom.

Gandhi spends a total of 2,338 days of his life in jail.

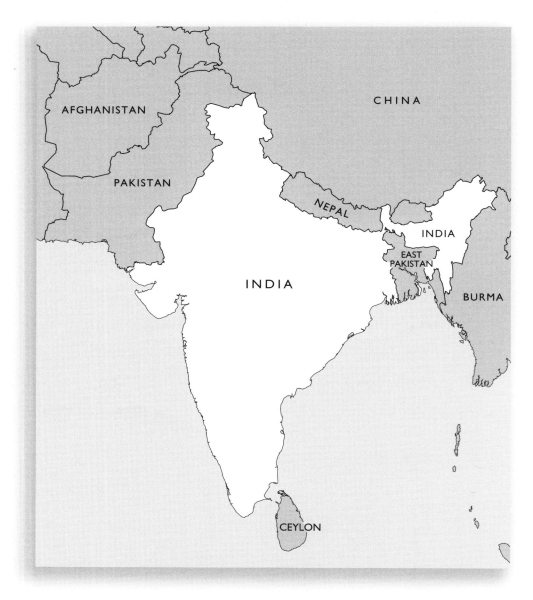

India and Pakistan

Gandhi's Protests

In 1947, India gains freedom from British rule. Gandhi wants one India. This does not happen. Many Hindus and Muslims do not want to live together. India splits into two countries. This splits makes many people angry. An angry Hindu man kills Gandhi.

Gandhi is shot on January 30, 1948.

In Hindu tradition, bodies are burned on a funeral **pyre**.

Gandhi's body is burned.

Gandhi's Flame

Gandhi stood for truth. Gandhi stood for justice. Gandhi stood for non-violence. Gandhi's body is burned on a fire. The fire burned out long ago. But Gandhi's flame still warms the world. Gandhi made the world a better place.

Mahatma Gandhi
1869 – 1948

Glossary

ashram: a spiritual community.

caste: a division or class of society.

protest: to complain about something.

pyre: a pile of wood for burning a dead body.

racism: a belief that one race is superior to others.

satyagraha: non-violent resistance.

symbol: an act that stands for an idea.

untouchable: a member of the lowest class of people in India.

Talking About the Book

What did you learn about Mahatma Gandhi?

What did you learn about India?

Describe Gandhi's beliefs.

Do you think Gandhi practiced what
he preached?

How did Gandhi make the world a better place?

Picture Credits